SOLD!
subject to contract

PAUL CAMPBELL
The Property Guru

Sold!
© Paul Campbell.

ISBN: 978-1-906316-33-4

All rights reserved.

Published in 2009 by HotHive Books, Evesham, UK.
www.thehothive.com

The right of Paul Campbell to be identified as the author of this work has been asserted by
him in accordance with the Copyright, Designs and Patents Act 1988.

A CIP record of this book is available from The British Library.

No part of this publication may be reproduced in any form or
by any means without prior permission from the author.

Printed in the UK by TJ International, Padstow.

SOLD!

subject to contract

ABOUT THE AUTHOR

About the author

Paul Campbell is a successful independent estate agent and property coach in Daventry, Northamptonshire. His refreshingly honest and down-to-earth advice is backed by 25 years of experience selling every kind of property imaginable, even during the downturn in the late 1980s.

Paul started his career as an estate agent at the age of 17. His enthusiasm for property combined with his empathetic nature and drive to excel at customer service means he has a strong grasp of what customers want when buying, selling and letting property – and then finding ways to get it for them.

There is no property matter he hasn't experienced or doesn't understand, and is well-qualified to help both novices and experts alike.

He set up his agency – Campbells – during the recession of the 1980s and since then has built his reputation to become a well-known and respected figure in the local community. He is regularly approached for comment and opinions by local and regional radio, TV and newspapers. Visit Paul's website at www.campbells-online.co.uk or find him on Facebook.

SOLD!

subject to contract

ACKNOWLEDGEMENTS

Acknowledgements

A book is always a huge undertaking and there is a cast of characters without which it simply wouldn't have happened...

A huge thank you has to go to Richard Wilkins and Liz Ivory – very very special people without whom I would never have had the guts to write this book in the first place.

Then there's Pete Farley and Sarah Collins who both took the time to be my 'Devil's Advocate' and whose honesty continually challenged me. I'm secretly really chuffed that I managed to change Pete's point of view about estate agents!

A big thank you must go to my associates Sue Berry, Mark Heycock, Jenny Ponder, Stan French, Angela Frank and Judy Seal. They've helped me make Campbells the great place it is, not to mention put up with me over the years!

To Becky Mattacola for her constant support and encouragement – you are amazing.

A thank you must go to my clients and associated professionals who have trusted me over the last 25 years and have given me so much research which has enabled me to both further my passion for selling property and now to write about it.

Finally, my thanks and appreciation must go to the people who have made the book a reality, Karen Swinden for helping me to write it; Cara Carey for pushing me hard to get everything done on time, friend and professional photographer Dawn Brannigan of www.shotatdawn.com, for being endlessly patient as I fidgeted constantly while she took shots for the front cover, and my father Sinclair Campbell and again Sarah Collins for taking the time to read through the manuscript at each stage and comment.

What people say about *Sold!*

"Paul tells it like it is! This book couldn't have come at a better time, when millions of sellers are trying desperately to sell their properties against a backdrop of falling prices and reticent buyers. This important, illuminating book will guide sellers through the perils and pitfalls of selling successfully during a recession."

Nigel Vokes (Director), Independent Solutions – providers of HIPs

"How to sell your property…guaranteed!" succeeds on two levels. If you've never sold a property before, it offers a comprehensive guide to the process involved, the techniques good estate agents use to market and sell a property, and the important role a seller should play in the process. If you've sold a property before and had a bad experience – as many have – you'll be thanking Paul for providing insider information on how to test an estate agent and pick the best. A back-to-basics tool for everyone who has a sell a property and doesn't know whether to be excited or dread it."

Peter MacKay, Managing Director of Expert Agent –
providers of estate agency web based software

"Sold! is a must read for anyone trying to sell or thinking about selling their property. Paul's written a practical and insightful guide which shows you how to sort the good agents from the bad, get a property looking its best and get the most money possible whatever the market conditions."

Julian O'Dell, TM Training and Development –
one of the UK's leading estate agency training providers

Contents

SOLD!

subject to contract

INTRODUCTION

Introduction

I began writing this book in early 2009. I was on Facebook one day, updating my status explaining that I was going through the final stages of my manuscript, when someone commented: "How are you going to write a book on that?" Many people assume that all you need to do to sell a house is put up a board, put together a description and photographs of the property and give the details to prospective buyers. You then put the whole lot up onto the web and – bingo! – your house is sold.

Going back even further to when I first started my career in property some 25 years ago, people thought agents just put up a 'For Sale' board, put your property in the window and then put it in the filing cabinet.

Selling property is much more complicated than that – well it is if you want to get a good price in a reasonable amount of time. To be good at it, you need many different skills, from understanding all the processes involved (such as valuations, HIPs, negotiation, project management, property law and finance) through to being focused on people and their problems, and even at times offering them counselling.

I have discovered over the years that both sellers and buyers need support and motivation from someone with inside knowledge of all aspects of property. Often people are selling their property under difficult circumstances – moving jobs, separating, having children, facing financial difficulties or downsizing because the house is too expensive or too hard to maintain (and these are just a few scenarios). Managing these situations requires good listening skills, the ability to sense when the seller is not really sure about moving and the ability to make everyone trust you and look to you for help, support and advice.

Moving house is considered to be one of the most stressful things you can do – up there with changing jobs and divorce. And for many sellers in today's market, their property feels like a millstone around their necks. The problem is that many sellers don't have a clear understanding of how the process works. Being a first-time seller can be as difficult as being a first-time buyer. But it doesn't have to be a painful process. Unfortunately, not all estate agents share my view and this is why for many sellers it can be an absolute nightmare.

My career started as an office boy in a financial services company, advising clients on how to get a mortgage for a property. I was 16 and responsible for making the coffee. I was also doing all the quotes on my typewriter and providing information to the consultant on interest rates and capital repayments. I also learned all about life assurance and pensions. I was the office dogsbody but, boy, did I learn a lot – although I didn't realise it at the time.

But I got fed up with running the office and applied for a job with an estate agency. I got the job because while I was being interviewed by the agent his secretary came in and said: "Your mortgage appointment is here." And he said: "Oh sugar, I haven't done the quotes." And I said: "What companies do you deal with? Give me a calculator and a rate card and I'll do it for you." And I got the job just like that.

He didn't even ask me if I had a full driving licence and that was one of the specifications for the job. My only means of transport was my trusted pushbike!

I quickly learned several things: how to deal with customers in the right way and how to arrange finance for purchases by finding the best ways of borrowing money. It was very much an unlicensed industry at that point.

I also learned about endowments, pensions and term assurance. I started working with both buyers and sellers and quickly became involved in everything from conveyancing to taking building society managers out to lunch to persuade them to release funds to borrowers. In those days, building societies had to wait for the money to come in from their savers before they could release it. We've now gone full circle and once again lenders are struggling not only to find funds but also to find ways to release them.

So I set out to do my first viewings and valuations on my bike. I was so embarrassed about it that I would park it around the corner, lock it to a lamp post and then walk to the appointment. Sometimes I forgot to take off my cycle clips!

Motivation must have been high on my agenda at that very young age. I remember pedalling as fast as I could to a viewing five miles from my office. I knew how long it would take because it was in my home village of Long Buckby. As I crawled up the steep hill past the station, my clients overtook me in their car waving as they went. It was my first sale and as my clients wanted the property so badly, I cycled back to the office to complete the mortgage form and then cycled back home for dinner. The passion for creating sales is still in my belly.

Eventually I got involved in building and renovating houses. My boss had that as a sideline. I used to work on the new houses at the weekends and on my days off when I didn't have a lot of money – I got paid to be a labourer. During the week, I got used to greeting people such as building control inspectors, architects and planners. I never realised at the time that I was soaking up information like a sponge and that it would come in so handy later.

We had some serious competition within the town, so I also had to learn very quickly about the other estate agencies and why they were doing better than us. I took the view that we had to find out what they were doing that we weren't. I used to follow them around and find out why they were getting more instructions than I was. I knew I had to learn better ways to get new business and within a short space of time we were the busiest estate agency in town and proud of it.

And then the last recession kicked in, sales figures started to fall and I got blamed for the poor results. Looking back, it was the market but we didn't recognise that at the time. So I had a big falling-out with the boss and I walked away.

I was 19 years old and jobless. I decided to continue working as a mortgage consultant from home but, if I am being honest, I was really struggling. That period of my life taught me a massive lesson. I was no longer networking. I was no longer seeing my future clients face to face because I had no office. I was hidden away at home relying on a phone and fax machine and, of course, it never rang. Advertising alone is not enough. So, I religiously walked around my home town pretending I was busy and had a lot to do. I started to get business because I was bumping into people I knew who wanted to speak to me. I didn't realise it at the time but people loved my motivation and passion for property. Christmas that year was creeping up fast and I knew I wouldn't have enough money to buy presents and I was already in debt to the mortgage company. Fear started to kick in.

A good friend of mine was working for a light haulage firm and he suggested that I could earn money from driving. So I started driving a seven and a half tonne lorry full of fridge freezers back and forth to Glasgow. In those days there were no mobile phones, only public phone boxes; people knew you were calling from them because of the beeps. So I got hold of a Little Chef map and a load of BT phone cards. That way I was able to phone my mortgage customers and lenders during the day from a Little Chef and because I was using a phone card no one knew I was using a public phone. I slept in the lorry at night to save money on digs and kept both jobs running at the same time. What a wicked experience – and one I will never forget!

One day in Northampton I met Ian, the guy who'd helped me with the mortgages back when I was an office boy working for the financial services company. He asked me what I was doing and I said: "Well, I am still a mortgage consultant and I have kept my Legal & General licence so I am still able to arrange mortgages."

He was working for an estate agency across the road and invited me to go and have a look at it. It was a family-run firm and the father had obviously set it up for his sons and Ian was working for them. Unfortunately, the business wasn't doing very well and the family were looking to sell it.

And of course, me being me, I said: "I'll buy it", even though I hardly had any money. I invited Ian to come and work for me. I couldn't buy it outright so I agreed to pay over a period of time. I obviously needed some money on top of this to keep running the business. I quickly wrote a business plan and rang my solicitor and said: "I need some money now, where can I get it from?" He recommended a bank manager based in Rugby and told me to put on my best suit. The bank actually lent me £25,000, although not all up front. It was enough to buy the furniture, a typewriter, a photocopier and a window display.

And so Campbell Estate Agency was born. I later shortened it to Campbells. Today, it is still an independent estate agency based in Northamptonshire offering property services in Daventry and the surrounding villages. We also advertise property all over the UK and overseas.

Northampton is the largest market town in the country and back in the 1980s was saturated with estate agencies. The key issue for me was how to win more business. It was a huge problem. I decided that really good customer service was the key and this meant not taking on any house for any fee. Some estate agencies 'stack 'em high' – they have hoards of properties and are prepared to drop their fees to any level just to get the business. This makes it impossible for them to concentrate properly on selling any of them and they survive by hoping that the properties will sell themselves. In the current climate and for a long time to come, this strategy is a mistake as you will see later in this book. Also you have to question any agencies that are prepared to drop their fees. What happens when they come to negotiate the price of your property with your buyer – will they be only too willing to drop your price as well?

In the late 1990s, I bought a rental business with the help of a silent partner. I had been after this business for six years as it was in Daventry, a town I knew very well. It was there that I learned everything I needed to know about lettings and property management. When I took over the business, there were unsigned leases, rental arrears and inspections that had not been carried out. I quickly learned to see the world from both perspectives: the landlord's and the person renting.

Eventually I turned the lettings agency into a full-blown estate agency, transferring the business from Northampton to focus on the Daventry area instead.

While I was running the lettings agency, I also set up a maintenance business. I had lots of maintenance issues to deal with. You name it, I had to fix it. I had to find someone to do every single job from a minor leak to a burst pipe and major flood. Any work that needed doing on the rental property I could subcontract to the maintenance business. This taught me valuable lessons in terms of dealing with subcontractors. I sold off the company several years ago, but I know how to sort out maintenance issues or find help with dressing a property. For example, I helped a client find a contractor to sort out fencing to improve the look of his garden. And recently, I refurbished a five-bed detached house for a client who I never met as he lived and worked in Dubai. I sold that property within weeks of it being refurbished for far more that it would have achieved if we had just sold it off. A good agent should be able to help buyers with any maintenance issues that need to be put right before a property goes onto the market.

I also have my own property portfolio and have refurbished hundreds of properties. During the course of this refurbishment work, I have learned about everything from getting planning permission from the local council through to redecorating, landscaping gardens, plumbing, electrics and replacing roofs.

In 2003, I launched a magazine called *Property Matters* and learned about the importance of selling locations not houses. One of the key features of the Northampton/Daventry area is the Grand Union Canal, and we would often feature these benefits.

One great example of this was when I sold a property based on a photograph of someone jumping on a train at the local railway station (good old Long Buckby station – I love it). You need to capture people's imaginations: if someone needs to commute every day to work and you have a property near a railway station, show how easy it would be to do this if they lived in that property. So, we regularly featured properties based not only on their best benefits but their location.

The magazine was hand delivered and placed in pubs, doctors' and dentists' surgeries – anywhere where people would pick it up and browse through it. In the end, I had to scale down the publication – it was too much to do. But it taught me an important lesson: selling property is about capturing the imagination of the buyer.

Around the same time, I set up a mortgage centre. I did this by accident. A shop became vacant on the high street and I didn't want another estate agency to set up there. I wasn't sure what to do with the shop at first but then decided to set up the Daventry Mortgage Centre. It was unusual at that time to find a mortgage broker on the high street; they were normally tucked away in an office somewhere.

I kept it for a few years and then sold it to a fellow director. In that time, however, I learned everything there is to know about financing a property purchase. I also learned what was going on in a customer's head when undertaking a property transaction. And those lessons are still applicable today. I still spend a lot of time with my own mortgage adviser, keeping abreast of the latest lending developments.

Having learned every aspect of the residential property market, I recently became a property coach. My aim is to get any property I take on to the top of a buyer's or prospective tenant's list. The purpose of this book is to help sellers choose the right agent or coach to ensure that their sale is as pain free as possible and that they get the best price for their property as quickly as possible.

I'm a great believer in certainty. Buying and selling property is much easier to handle if you can start enjoying that moment you have been waiting for – either completion of a sale or purchase or both. It doesn't matter what happens in the middle because it will never go the way it's planned but, trust me, it is much easier if you have someone by your side who can coach you through the different emotional and sometimes challenging events. It's never that easy but picture the day of completion and you will get there.

SOLD!

subject to contract

CHAPTER 1
MARKET CONDITIONS

Market conditions

When the property market was booming, many houses just sold themselves. Not any more. The housing market is very demanding, and agencies that don't pull their finger out and really market a client's property will find themselves with very demotivated staff and probably no clients at all.

Already, large numbers of them have gone out of business. About 50% of all UK property pages are viewed on Rightmove – making it the largest property website in the UK. According to Rightmove, 20% of estate agencies went bust in 2008.

We are no longer in a seller's market – at one point in 2008 there were 15 homes for every buyer. So, as a seller in a tough market, you can't afford to end up with an agent who doesn't understand how to find and hold on to those elusive buyers. Only the best agencies, those who are committed to going the extra mile for customers, will get through the next few tough years.

Marketing property takes a lot more than just sticking a sign in front of your house and putting it online; in fact, anyone can do that. It takes innovative marketing to sell your property and you need to ask some searching questions to find the agent who can do the job properly. See Chapter 3 for how to choose the right agent or property coach.

A buyers' market

According to the website, HousePrices.uk.net, the number of houses bought and sold each month in England and Wales used to be about 100,000, based on government figures. However, during the second half of 2008 that figure fell each month and by December it was as low as 56,000.

The main reasons are:

- Difficulties in getting mortgages due to the credit crunch (mortgage lenders have no money for buyers to borrow)

- The economic recession and rising unemployment

- Concerns about getting into the housing market while house prices are falling.

However, since the peak in July 2009, UK house prices have fallen considerably and new buyers are starting to show more interest in the market. There are certainly more first-time buyers around and they could play a part in the recovery of the market as they represent a build-up in pent-up demand. Since 2003, first-time buyers have been responsible for only 33% of transactions, compared to an average of 46% since 1979. According to Fionnuala Earley, Nationwide's chief economist, this adds up to about 750,000 buyers between 2003 and 2007.

This pool of first-time buyers could make its way back into the market when houses become more affordable for them. We are also starting to see families guaranteeing loans. The 55-plus age group is the richest band of people in the country. They have been scripted to save so they are cash and asset rich. Many are sitting on good-size properties, have paid off their mortgages and have money in the bank. These first-time buyers are doing deals with their parents and getting them to invest in their first property. Let's face it, investing a capital lump sum in a property is a far better long-term prospect than anything else at the moment.

Not only are there signs that the first-time buyer market is growing, first-time buyers are also buying bigger properties than would be expected because of falling prices. Some first-time buyers are even looking at four-bed properties.

There is no doubt that prices will start to level out, but buyers will still remain in control of the market. The one lesson to learn from this as a seller is to keep an eye on the market to see who is buying properties like yours – you may find the market is changing and you will need to think about how to present your property to a different type of buyer than the one you expected.

So, what should a seller do?

As house prices fall and the number of houses being sold diminishes, the market has swung away from being in favour of the seller to putting buyers in a much stronger position. It is, therefore, essential for sellers to understand how to get their property to the top of a buyer's list and choosing the right estate agency is more important than ever.

We are used to thinking that when we buy or sell a house we can make lots of money. TV programmes such as Location, Location, Location have conditioned us to think of our house as a property investment rather than our home. It is no longer possible or relevant to do this.

As a seller, you need to be much more realistic about the value of your house. When you hear statistics about house prices, for example from the Land Registry, remember that they are based on information that is several months old. Often sellers are playing catch-up and this can have a massive impact on their ability to sell their house.

This is where a good estate agent comes in. They will have researched the market and seen what else is available to buyers in the area and at what prices. Listen to what they have to say about pricing. Just because a similar house to yours sold a few months ago at a higher price, it doesn't mean yours will fetch the same money. The market is constantly changing and it is important to keep up to date. The right estate agent will work with you and keep you appraised of the latest market conditions.

Negative equity

Many people believe that if they are in negative equity it is impossible to sell their property. This is not necessarily the case. In the US, it is better known as short sale, which is an agreement where a lender accepts less than the amount owed on a property when it's sold because unacceptable hardship means the borrower cannot make payments any more.

In the UK, lenders are now willing to take less for the property than is owed on it because it would be worth even less if they had to repossess and auction it off. The shortfall is then carried over and the borrower agrees terms to pay off the outstanding balance of the mortgage over a period of time. This does mean, of course, that the borrower will need to move into rental accommodation until they have paid off the outstanding amount but it is all possible and makes life a lot easier.

A good estate agent or property coach should be able to explain how a short sale works if you are in negative equity. It is vitally important that you don't leave it until the last minute; talk to someone as soon as possible. They should also be able to negotiate on your behalf with your lender. If you find yourself in this situation, remember not to panic and make sure you keep up your monthly mortgage repayments above all else. You will make life much more difficult for yourself if you start negotiation off on the wrong footing.

Also there is a growing trend among lenders in the UK to encourage borrowers to remortgage with other lenders, therefore releasing money back for them to lend to other customers.

State of mind

Another key issue for sellers is state of mind. There is no point in sitting and worrying for hours and hours about whether your property will sell. Choose to think positively and enjoy that certainty. Your property will sell. Instead, concentrate your energy on making the property look as good as possible and following the steps outlined in the action plan at the end of the following chapter.

I had a client called Howard who was moving to a new job in Sheffield. He was worrying about every aspect of the move and rang me nearly every day to talk about his concerns. I had to tell him to stop worrying about the sale – let me do that – and concentrate instead on his new job. It is important to let things take their natural course and if you don't trust your agent to get on with your sale then you need to choose a better one.

The housing market may have slowed down considerably, but there are still buyers out there. Don't look down; look ahead. If you are depressed, that will show itself in the house and create a bad feeling. Your house has got to have a good feeling. A poor ambience can lose you thousands of pounds.

I remember visiting a client where the lady of the house had multiple sclerosis and her husband was trying to keep his wife happy. Sadness permeated the house and viewers were picking up on this. During viewings, I suggested that the lady sat out in the garden while the husband went out. I turned on the radio before each viewing – simple things can really help improve the ambience of a property. As a result of these small changes, there was no more negativity in the house and viewers saw the lady enjoying the garden. The house soon sold.

So the key to getting your house sold is to choose the right agent, listen to their advice on pricing and presentation and keep a positive mental attitude. Just remember there is a buyer out there waiting to find your property!

This book is a guide to finding an agency that will really work hard on your behalf and ensure that you get your house to the top of that buyer's list. It also teaches sellers how to keep control of the process by taking it one stage at a time, and provides hints and tips on how to understand what a buyer is looking for and improve the look of your property accordingly.

You may find me stating the obvious at times but, if you do all the things I suggest, I guarantee you will attract those buyers.

SOLD!

subject to contract

CHAPTER 2
REASONS FOR SELLING

Reasons for selling

There are many different reasons why someone wants to sell their property. It could be that they need to save money and want to move somewhere smaller, less expensive to run or to a cheaper location. On the other hand, it could be a second-time buyer who wants somewhere bigger – especially now that property prices have fallen.

Other reasons include people moving due to work. They may have a new job in a new location. It could be parents buying a property for their son or daughter. It could be a couple going through a separation and needing to sell to buy two separate properties or it could be someone selling a property for a deceased relation.

During my 30 years of selling property, I have learned that there is a different story behind each sale. One client came to see me and told me that I had been recommended by a friend. He was off to Australia and wanted me to sell his property. I never saw him again. He handed me the keys and asked me to keep him informed by email at every stage and that's how I sold his house for him.

I was once asked by the Court of Protection to sell a property on behalf of an old man who had been in an institution for 18 years and his assets were being looked after by the Government. My role was to act on behalf of him and the Government, although he didn't know his house was for sale.

I picked up the keys from the institution and drove to his house. I couldn't get through the front door because the hallway was full of post. It rapidly became obvious that no one had been in the house for 18 years – there were still bottles in the fridge and plates on the table. I arranged for an auction house to take away all the contents and then put the house up for sale. That was a huge job to do, but it had to be done.

One of the most difficult situations I have encountered was a family in considerable stress. The grandmother had a heart condition, her son was losing his business and the grandson had had brain surgery and had a ragged scar across the top of his head. I did all I could to make the sales process as pain free as possible by discussing a plan of action with them so that everyone was happy.

On another occasion, I had to deal with a deceased estate and I had 18 beneficiaries to satisfy. They were all over the world and we didn't have email then. It was a nightmare but again it had to be done.

While reasons for moving are many and varied, one thing is certain: there will always be an element of emotion involved in the process.

Emotions

Don't underestimate the importance of feelings in the decision to move house, particularly the emotional baggage that comes with separation, or uprooting the family to a new location.

Selling a house as a result of a family break-up can often be difficult and requires an agent who is capable of mediation, otherwise the whole thing can fall apart. Often the couple are no longer speaking to each other. The only way to progress is to get them both to agree to sell by making them understand that it's in both of their interests to do so. In these cases, it is important to understand what clients are going through and help them come to the right conclusion about the sale.

Every client has different problems, issues or goals. A father buying a house for his son wants the son to like the property but it must also be a good investment for the father. There can be tension between those two goals.

Clients may not know what they're doing and will need help, sometimes even figuring out what they really want to achieve. An estate agent who is really a property coach will slot everything together to help the client feel better, rather than just not asking any questions and putting the house straight on the market.

One thing I have learned throughout my 20 years' experience is that people often don't reveal their emotional stress about moving. The most important thing is to find out what the client really wants to achieve; getting the full story can prevent false starts.

For example, I went to see one client and asked them: "Why do you want to sell your house?" Their reply was that they wanted to move somewhere else. "So you're not happy where you are?" I asked them. "Well we've got two dogs and a small yard."

"OK," I said, "so do you really want to move?" It was at this point that the uncertainty emerged.

My response in these situations is always to say: "I'm happy to come round and do a quick valuation to give you a ballpark figure of what your house is worth, but I think you would be wasting time and money trying to sell your house now."

If the client's main reason is to better their personal living, I suggest refurbishing instead. If it is because they need more space, the amount a client saves on not moving house could be put towards an extension, and in a few years' time the market might be better for selling it. When you come to sell, refurbishing or extending your house will help you to sell. Meanwhile, it is providing you with the home you want.

So, before you start dealing with an estate agent, you need to know what you're trying to achieve and you should explain that in full to get the best advice. Before you begin the process of selling, ask yourself some key questions:

- What am I trying to achieve?

- How quickly?

- When do I want to move and what are the reasons behind this?

- What are my expectations?

- How much do I really know about the process?

- Why not leave it to my estate agent or property coach to manage for me?

Even the most seasoned seller thinks they know all there is to know about selling. Unfortunately, many of them carry forward bad experiences from the past and dread the prospect of selling again. I often tell my clients to write down everything they are worried about, even when they wake up in the middle of the night.

You especially need to be honest if your mortgage is higher than the value of the house, and ask yourself "What can I get?" rather than say "What I want is…"

Timing

Having established that the client is serious about moving, the next key question is one of time: how quickly do they need to move and how much time is there to get the property to the top of a buyer's list?

If a client is having another child, the key question is when is the baby due? When will the property become a problem? The answer could be when the child is six months old or more, when it needs its own bedroom. That gives you the time frame in which to work.

You must be realistic about the price, especially if you need to sell sooner rather than later. I had one client whose father had died leaving her and her sisters his bungalow. I recommended that they sold it as quickly as possible; the alternative was to stick out for a higher price. Meanwhile, they had to pay the running costs on the property and risk leaving it empty. They took the view that it was better to sell sooner at a realistic price and, within two weeks, it had sold and for the asking price.

If a client is in debt or negative equity, going through a separation or having to relocate, then they need an agent who will help them to sell their property as quickly as possible.

In the past, I've helped people move on from unpleasant situations, especially if they're being threatened by repossession. The right action at the right time can prove pivotal to prevent clients being blacklisted by creditors for many years. My experience stems directly from helping desperate sellers during the market downturn in the 1990s. With the right agent, clients turn around a desperate situation, especially if debt collectors are calling and bankruptcy seems inevitable. Unfortunately, I don't know any other estate agent prepared (or knowledgeable enough) to help its customers in this way.

You have to accept the fact that, if you want to sell something, it has to go at the correct price or it simply won't go. If you are in negative equity, for example, negotiate terms with your lender so that you can put your house on the market for a realistic price rather than try to sell it at too high a price. You need to sell it and get out so you don't have to keep paying your unaffordable mortgage!

Another issue to factor into selling your property is moving costs. These can range from £5,000 to £10,000 depending on the size of house. One of my colleagues did an estimate for a client that came out at £20,000, including extra work that needed to be done on the new house (new kitchen, bathroom, windows, blinds, carpets and so on). So many expenses run off the back of moving. It's not an issue as long as you make sure it's written in your plan.

ACTION PLAN

Having made the decision to move, there are a number of steps you need to take in selling the property – don't try to do them all at once. We have already discussed quite a few of these, such as choosing the right agent, timing and pricing.

Some clients are very organised and have everything planned out, others leave everything to the last minute. So, what needs to go into the action plan?

- How fast do you want to move?

- Do you sell your house privately or use an estate agency?

- Which estate agency do you use?

- How do you price your property?

- What are the key benefits of the property
  (essential for marketing purposes)?

- How should you best present your house?

- What alterations do you need to make/jobs do you need to finish
  (such as moving furniture, filling in holes and painting)?

- How will viewings take place?

- How will people perceive your property from the street
  (for example, do you need to weed the garden, repaint the
  front door, clean the windows)?

- Do you need to declutter? If you had to move today, what would
  you leave behind?

- Where are you going to market the property?

The following chapters will help you answer these questions. The key one, without a doubt, is getting the right agent because they will advise you on how to price your property, how to present and market it, and how best to undertake viewings and negotiate with potential buyers. But before you choose your estate agent, read on!

SOLD!

subject to contract

CHAPTER 3
CHOOSING THE RIGHT ESTATE AGENT

Choosing the right estate agent

So, let's assume you really don't want to get involved in selling your own property. You decide you need to bite the bullet and employ an estate agent to do it for you. What's the best way to go about this?

Do your research

I was helping a friend a few years ago to sell a property in Newcastle. I began my research by looking on the internet to see which agencies operated in that area of town so they would have the best local knowledge. I rang five of them to see how they behaved over the phone. Did they have a good telephone manner, were they helpful, did they ask the right questions to understand exactly what I was looking for and what I was trying to achieve? Could I work closely with this company?

You should judge an estate agency by the person who answers the phone. It's like the front of house in a restaurant. If the glasses and cutlery are dirty, what does the kitchen look like? People usually choose an agency based on the person who initially comes to see them. But this isn't giving you the whole picture: for example, if the administrator doesn't run the estate agency practice efficiently then the whole process won't work.

Having done the research, I drew up my shortlist of agencies and then drove up to Newcastle to visit them with the aim of finding out which was the best one I could work with. It really is important to be able to work together with your agent. I began by looking at each agency's window. Was it clean and well presented? Were there good photographs of properties? Did they jump out at me and encourage me to ask for more information? I then entered the office and in one case found an agent eating a hamburger at his desk, making the entire room smell. Would I want a potential buyer to experience this? Did I get the feeling I wanted to go in? If I didn't, my buyer wouldn't either.

My next test was to see whether they would ask me the right questions. You need to have an agent who is interested in you and who you are – they should be establishing what it is that you are trying to achieve. A key test is whether they make you feel special. Have they understood your anxieties/ expectations? If not, how will they treat your prospective buyers?

So, to find the best agent, remember to do your research. Start with the web to find out who your local agencies are and how they market themselves. Choose the best five, phone them and then pay them a visit. As you do this, put yourself in the mindset of your buyer. A final question you must ask your prospective estate agent is: "Apart from yourself, who do you consider to be the best agent to sell my property?" Now, that is an interesting question. Trust me, out of the five agents you ask, there will always be one who will shine above the rest for customer service.

You need to make absolutely sure that your agent has the ethics, experience, marketing and internet knowledge, and 'skill set' that it takes to market your home effectively. It makes sense when you're working flat out or busy taking care of your family to have an estate agent who is working hard in the background on your behalf. You can't afford to end up with an agent who does the bare minimum and doesn't understand how to find the buyers. If you choose the wrong agent, you will lose money.

New ways to market properties

In today's fast-moving life, many buyers simply do not use the traditional ways of looking for a property. Long gone are the days of picking up the local newspaper and trawling through the property pages or taking a day off to visit estate agencies. Now they use the internet and email. A survey I carried out found that 97% of my clients wanting to buy a property want to communicate via the internet and email. Don't get me wrong, the local newspaper has its place but you have to find an agency that understands how a buyer thinks and behaves.

Your expectations as a buyer may be very different from a prospective buyer's. If you want to find your buyer as quickly as possible, your agent must be able to react positively to these expectations. So make sure they have an emailing list as well as active telemarketing. I can't reiterate this enough. Sending wads of paper-based sales particulars in an envelope will be a thing of the past very shortly – and rightly so because it is very time consuming, costly and environmentally wasteful.

Over 97% of my customers want and are happy for me to forward information by email. 'Click and delete' is the term I use. It's instant and it can be read and stored at your prospective buyer's convenience on their PC and now on the latest smart phones.

When your property hits the market, you need to tell as many buyers as possible and the best ones are those who are already talking to your local 'best' agent! I use this method, working alongside a company called www.expertagent.co.uk. Every single quality buyer I have is connected to this system and at a click of a button I can email information and pictures straight into my buyers' inboxes or their PCs or mobile phones. Not only that, I can update all of the buyers every week with the latest property and mortgage information, price changes and new instructions just in case they have missed or discarded a particular property.

As well as excellent photographs, I send virtual tours via a link and website links to help my buyers make more informed decisions.

Ask all of the agents you interview how they will be sending information about your property to potential buyers. Make sure you use an agent who works with www.expertagent.co.uk or similar. If you don't, you really are going to struggle to find enough interest in your property; if you do, you will inevitably get more viewings and more offers.

Top tips to find the best agent

Here are the ten other tips that should help you choose the best agent:

1. **Establish how long the agent has been in business.**
   This gives a basic indication of their experience and ability to survive the ups and downs in the marketplace. However, it doesn't necessarily indicate that they're an active seller. They may have been in business for ten years, but they may have sat back on their established name, whereas another agent who's been in business for two years may be really motivated and eager to please – after all, they have a lot more to gain.

   The agency may be long established but how long have the staff been working there? Do they have experience of anything other than a seller's market or are they just order-takers?

2. **Look at the professional organisations they belong to.**

   Estate agency is an unregulated industry and open to abuse. Anyone can become an estate agent. They don't need any qualifications and there are no mandatory regulations that estate agents must abide by, in contrast to financial advisers regulated by the Financial Services Authority (FSA). Any estate agent you choose should, as a minimum, be a member of the National Association of Estate Agents (NAEA) and Ombudsman for Estate Agents (OEA), which requires members to work within their codes of practice.

3. **Ask them how many homes they've sold to completion in the past six months.**

   Many agencies rely on large numbers of 'Sold' boards to demonstrate their capabilities, but these are no indication of whether the sale of a property actually reached completion, just that it is going though the sales process. A good agent will know the figures and have no hesitation in telling you. A poor agent will either not know, will not want you to know or will just make it up! Ask them for comparables.

4. **What commission do they charge?**

   Low commissions are not a good sign: they have to take on a high volume of houses to reach a certain level of profitability and you can expect little, if any, service as a result. In this case, what seemed at the outset to be a bargain may ultimately cost you much more than you planned to spend in money, time and stress. If you are paying a higher commission, such as 2%, you have the right to complain about poor service from your agent. If you have a discounted rate, it is much harder to complain. What does a low fee say about the agent's confidence and negotiating skills? I would rather pay just that little bit more for an agent that was going to perform, stick up for me and negotiate a higher sale price.

5. **How does the agent find prospective buyers?**

In today's marketplace, there are only so many buyers out there who are ready and able to purchase a property. When you enter the market to sell, you enter one of the most competitive businesses in existence. In a good market, competition is fierce, ethics can be a rare commodity and, if you're not ready, your property just sits on the market. The agent you eventually choose has to identify potential buyers quickly, before other agents get to them and persuade them to buy a different property.

So, how does an agent identify these 'hot' prospects before the competition? How are they going to make the phone ring with lots of viewings for your property? This is what separates the weak agent from the shrewd. Your agent must have a powerful marketing strategy! Make sure you do your homework. Try finding similar properties to yours on the internet and consider which agency shone above the rest in terms of marketing.

The best agencies use every available marketing tool, technology, approach, contact or potential avenue to generate prospective buyers for your property. They understand the value of effective advertising and how to create ads that generate a response. They can't just fling their name out, sit back and expect people to call. Let's face it, all their ads look virtually the same anyway. So, what's unique about your agent that's going to grab prospects and get them to pick up the phone and call? They have to craft their ads to give prospects a compelling reason to call.

6. **Can you get hold of your agent when you need to?**

   Have you got their direct number and email address? A generic companywide email address – such as mail@joebloggs_EstateAgents.co.uk – isn't acceptable. You should be able to email and talk directly to the agent who is selling your property whenever you want to. At the very least, you should be able to talk to someone who knows who you are and about the property you're selling. There is nothing worse than ringing an agent's office and no one knows who you are. Establish from the start how you would like your agent to communicate with you. Would you like a weekly/monthly update or would you rather they only talk to you when something is happening? It's down to you to establish the ground rules and a good agent will contact you in the way that suits you best. It makes sense to work very closely with the whole office to get the best result.

   In a sense, you become like a member of the family during the process. I have one client who still comes in every week to say hello. We enjoy seeing her in the office – she is a very inspirational person and someone we all respect. How nice it would be to have your very own estate agent who you could genuinely recommend, in much the same way that we recommend dentists, solicitors and others.

7. **How good are the agent's negotiating skills?**

   This is a crucial part of the process, so you need to ask what kind of results have they produced for past clients? Check references. At the very least, talk to two or three of your agent's most recent clients. See what kind of effort they are making to get the job done. Their role is to get you, the seller, as much money as possible for your property. Unfortunately, a poor negotiator could lose you a sale let alone thousands of pounds. I am absolutely passionate about agents who work for the seller to get the last penny. I used to joke about this. Use me to sell your property but have your wits about you if you want to buy one from me. After all, who pays the fees?

Most people think that selling a property is like being a tour guide. Show the prospect around, ask if they like it and phone the seller to report back. Well, if that's all there was to it, anyone could sell your property. The agent you choose must have strong negotiating skills. Without them, you can never hope to get the highest possible price for what is normally your biggest asset.

The best agents can't wait to tell you all about the innovative methods that separate them from the agents who just poke a 'For Sale' sign in the ground and act as if that's enough! Give them the chance to tell you why they are different. I know it might seem boring but you should be thinking about your property from a buyer's perspective and not from your own.

8. **Look closely at what they value your house at and make sure you ask at least three estate agents in to value your property.**
The last thing you want is to be taken in by an agent promising to sell for more than your property is worth while you end up sitting on the sidelines watching everyone else sell before you. One more thing. Never tell an agent what another one valued your house at. Make them demonstrate their skills and work for your business. You don't have to be rude – just ask.

9. **Are they enthusiastic?**
Never take on an agent who appears bored or in a hurry or gives the impression that yours is just another instruction to add to the list. If they're willing to display those characteristics to you when they should be putting their best foot forward to win your confidence, they'll have no hesitation in putting off buyers with their shoddy attitude. They may also be the kind of agent who puts your security at risk by giving your house keys to buyers and sending them unaccompanied on viewings. (Yes, it does happen.)

10. Is the agent available at evenings and weekends?

Most buyers are working during the day and prefer to view houses in the evenings and at weekends. If your agent goes home at 6pm or only opens until midday on Saturdays, how are buyers going to see your property? For me, being available for my clients is absolutely essential and I can receive emails on my mobile phone so they can always contact me.

It's sad, I know, but I am passionate about my clients and I promise to be there when they need me most.

No minimum contract length

Having chosen your estate agent, you now need to look at their contract. Ordinarily, if you sign a sole agency contract you're obliged to stay with that agency for between 8 and 12 weeks, no matter how poorly they perform. Go for a multi-agency contract and you'll be hit by a bigger fee and the distinct impression that the agencies can't really be bothered to compete with each other to sell your property. Even worse, the Estate Agents (Provision of Information) Regulations 1991 require agents to 'make you aware' of their terms of business and, once they have done, it could be considered legally binding even if you haven't signed a contract!

Personally, I take a more flexible approach to contracts. Firstly, I discuss my terms of business with clients in detail to ensure they understand exactly what they mean, then I put everything we've discussed down on paper in clear, jargon-free English so clients know what to expect and there are no unpleasant surprises.

Secondly, I don't tie clients down to a minimum length of time. They are free to leave at any time if I don't meet their expectations. And, of course, I will only go ahead and market a client's property once they have signed on the dotted line giving me permission to do so. *Clients stay with me because they want to, not because they have to.*

So many consumers place estate agents on a pedestal. However, if you are not completely satisfied, then you should have the freedom to go somewhere else should you feel threatened or bullied. I can't tell you the number of times I have had to mentor a client to deal with this type of behaviour.

If you speak to any other agents, make sure the agent goes over every detail with you. Make sure the start and end dates are on the agreement. Know exactly what fees you will be paying, and remember, less is not always better.

Finally, if I do take on a client with a multi-agency agreement, I'm not going to leave the marketing to someone else in another agency. I make sure I'm the one to sell the property. If you find a really good estate agent, please give them sole agency. Good agents genuinely care about their clients. They do. I've spent years justifying assumptions that consumers make. Trust me on this one – choose the right agent using my advice and I promise you won't need to use more than one agent. For over 20 years, I have treated my sole agency instructions with the utmost priority. Those clients have relied on me to get them moved and on to the next chapter of their lives.

Don't get me wrong, those clients whose properties I have sold on a multi-agency instruction still get top service. But give me a sole agency challenge any day. Ask your agent what they think about these issues.

When it comes to fees, you get what you pay for

You may feel, like many other sellers, that the only way to differentiate between so many estate agencies that appear to offer similar services is to go with the one offering the lowest commission. More often than not this strategy backfires. Time and time again I see sellers losing literally thousands of pounds using a cheap agency.

Low commissions are only possible if corners are cut. There may be little or no sales training for their staff or after-sale support for you, which results in missed offers, a slower sale and a lower sale price. In these circumstances, why would anyone spend the time negotiating on your behalf for every penny?

You can usually spot them by the fact that they have early closing hours, little or no weekend and late evening viewings, no regular contact with their customers, photocopied (rather than nicely designed and printed) details with hard-to-see photos (if they have proper photos), scruffy-looking boards and newspaper adverts with pages and pages of houses all crammed into as small a space as possible.

To guarantee a certain level of profit in the business, agencies offering low commissions need to secure a high turnover of properties to keep going. With so many properties on their books, they simply don't have the time to ensure clients have the best possible care during one of the most stressful periods of their life. You really don't want your property just sitting there among a pile of others. I heard one agent describe his process as "throwing as much muck at the fan as possible and seeing what sticks". Please keep away from this type of agent – it's not healthy!

In addition, you will frequently find that these agencies place great importance on the number of boards they display. This is obviously no indication of how many properties have been successfully sold through to completion, only that the property is currently for sale or that the sales process has begun. The same applies to newspapers. Just because one agency saturates the newspaper with properties, it doesn't mean that your property will be easy to see. In fact, the reverse is likely to happen.

If you really are anxious about agents' fees, you can always offer them a money incentive (such as £1,000) if they sell your property. This will focus the agent's mind considerably and ensure that your details are on the top of the pile to show a prospective buyer. Remember if you do this, you must lay out exactly what you expect from them in return.

What is a property coach?

I have already mentioned the concept of a property coach several times in this book but would like to take the opportunity here to draw out the distinctions between an estate agent and a coach.

A property coach researches the market for your property by looking at the competition, the local area and what it offers, and looking at your property from the eyes of a buyer before they even view it.

In addition, they will have a look at the property at different times of the day (for example, school time and rush hour). They will walk around the neighbourhood and generally arm themselves with as much local knowledge as possible. They will also explore all the different avenues to get to the property so that when they accompany viewers they can bring them by the best route (past the shops, railway station, school and so on, depending on what the buyer is looking for).

Understanding market conditions

A property coach has to get the property to the top of a buyer's list. They do this by making sure the property is priced accordingly. Property portals, such as Rightmove, will give statistics on a particular area, such as how well/quickly houses are selling and for how much. Just be careful not to use information on the internet that is out of date. A property coach will know what has been going on in the past three months and will be up to date with the latest trends and statistics, ensuring that the property is priced correctly for the market.

The key is to value the property realistically, based on a combination of its location, its condition and the current market conditions. There is nothing wrong with being optimistic about the selling price, but not to the point where it costs money and causes an immense amount of anxiety.

If your goal is to move quickly for the best price you can get, it doesn't make sense to 'add a bit extra' to the price, as this will simply slow down interest in your property. And the market today is so volatile that you could lose tens of thousands of pounds in a downturn just because of a lack of knowledge on the part of the agent. If the market dips and you stay above the line in the belief that it will sell, you will lose a lot of money in the long run when buyers see it as too expensive.

On the other hand, if you want to capitalise on the full market value of your property and you are under no pressure to move quickly, then a higher price for a longer time might work, but this isn't a tactic I would recommend. The trouble is that when you really do need to sell, will anyone take you seriously?

To ensure an accurate valuation, a property coach works out what your property will, realistically, be worth given the current market conditions and compared to other houses in your area. This involves monitoring the Land Registry database, obtaining comparable reports from the property portals and monitoring the sold prices of similar properties in the area.

The property coach will evaluate your property based on this research, its current condition and how well it is presented, including which features appear to add or detract from its value. Only then are you given a true value that reflects the prevailing market and makes it attractive to its target market.

Getting the presentation right

A good property coach will then ensure that the property is presented at its best. While they will compliment the seller on their home, they need to be honest and say what aspects of the décor may not be relevant to a buyer, no matter how much love the owner has put into them. Chapter 4 explains in more detail how best to present your property to attract the right buyer.

Having got the property looking its best, it is time to put together the particulars. These need to include excellent photographs and a really good description of the property, featuring its key benefits. The coach will ask the client to come up with a list of at least ten benefits of living in their house (close to a train station, near bars/pubs, restaurants and take-aways, schools and so on).

A coach is always thinking: "Why should the person looking at the details online view your property?" Most estate agents and sellers don't think along those lines at all; they think about themselves, their own preferences, perceptions and expectations. But it's really the person buying the property that matters. For more information on marketing your property, see Chapter 5.

SOLD!

subject to contract

CHAPTER 4
HOW TO PRESENT YOUR HOUSE

How to present your house

We all love our homes and find it hard when anyone criticises them. But everyone's taste is different and buyers, in particular, will be quick to find fault as they have a tendency to haggle over price.

Sellers often believe that buyers will see past their clutter, unfinished maintenance jobs and décor. Well they won't, and they will reduce your price accordingly. You need your estate agent to be open and frank about your property. This way you have a chance of putting right anything that needs doing to make it more marketable and to achieve the maximum possible asking price. Making the right improvements will make all the difference and can often be accomplished quite easily.

Unless they're looking for an investment property, buyers choose a home because it pushes a number of emotional buttons for them and they can see themselves living there, which is why good presentation of a property is half the battle in securing an offer.

While an agent can do everything to market your property, its saleability and, ultimately, its value, are down to you. Agents who tell you during the valuation not to bother doing anything because they've got buyers lined up and your property will fly out of the door are probably not telling the truth. Your house should be clean, tidy and presentable and you need to do everything you can to achieve this. If you are too busy, your agent should be able to recommend someone who can sort this out for you.

You can also make many changes that can give a prospective buyer better feelings about your property, by making it feel light and spacious, with plenty of storage space but also giving a sense of privacy, warmth and security. Basic, simple and inexpensive improvements can provide an improved emotional response in a potential buyer.

The well-known TV House Doctor, Ann Maurice, knows how to give buyers good vibes about a property yet what she does is very simple – make buyers imagine they could walk in off the street and enjoy living in the property without having to do anything to it.

So put yourself into the shoes of a buyer. Take a good, frank look at your house and imagine a buyer coming in for the first time. What will they see? This will enable you to put in place the right strategies to get your property to the top of a buyer's list.

In a buyers' market, you need to ensure that you don't give them an excuse to gazunder. Gazundering is where a prospective buyer makes an offer that the seller accepts, and then reduces the offer shortly before completion of the sale. The buyer is counting on the seller being eager to sell and reluctant to have to market their house all over again.

For example, the buyer presents an offer of £180,000 on a house to which the owner agrees, only for the buyer to then gazunder them by offering £150,000 just before final contracts are exchanged.

I know one example of a seller who got gazundered trying to sell a property in a very bad state. A poor quality property can often attract the worst kind of buyer. If the seller had listened to my advice and spent a little time and money making the property look better, he would have attracted a better kind of buyer.

Also, it never hurts to be on friendly terms with a buyer. If the buyer can see that the seller would be hurt by such actions, the buyer's conscience might stop them from attempting to gazunder.

And remember, you need to dress your house so that buyers fall in love with it. Imagine who your buyers might be. Are they:

- Empty nesters (couples wanting to downsize as their children have left home)

- Young professionals

- First-timers

- Growing families?

If they are growing families, they will want to see space for children to play. If they are young professionals, they will want power showers and contemporary kitchens.

So how do you present your property to ensure that it gets to the top of a buyer's list?

The street scene

The first thing to do is drive up outside your own house and look at it objectively. Is the outside (that is, the street scene) tidy? Have rubbish bins been put away, is the garden path clear of weeds and toys and has it been swept? Is the front door freshly painted and the door knocker gleaming? Are the windows clean and the curtains/blinds tidy?

A buyer will be put off in seconds by any signs of neglect or untidiness and they won't have even seen the inside of the property. On the other hand, a nicely planted front garden makes a buyer feel at home, and appeals to their vanity because everyone wants to live in an attractive house.

What about the houses next to you and in the rest of the street? If your neighbour's grass needs cutting, why not offer to do this while you cut yours? On one occasion, the neighbour had an old caravan parked on the grass right outside my client's lounge window! I spoke to the owner and discovered he couldn't afford to get someone to tow it away, so I arranged for it to be moved. I just had to make a polite enquiry.

Another example is when you are selling an apartment. Sometimes the communal areas need a tidy up or a quick lick of paint. It takes nothing really to do this. And why not place a vase of flowers on a window ledge?

Decluttering and cleaning

Get rid of everything you haven't used in ages or would throw away if you had to move tomorrow. Also remove very personal items, such as family photographs, as they stop buyers from thinking they could live in the property. Anything you haven't used for a few months and are unlikely to use just box up and put in the loft or store somewhere else.

Make sure that you don't have too much furniture in your rooms. Again, you can always put things into storage until you move.

It is absolutely essential that the property is spotlessly clean. Don't leave any dirty dishes in the kitchen or even clean dishes on the draining board. Put everything away and make sure your cupboards are clean – viewers will open them to see how much room there is inside. I know of one agent who hid a dirty frying pan in the oven. The buyer opened the oven and found it there and the owner couldn't find the pan for weeks! Make sure you deep clean the oven and hob and don't forget the extractor fan.

Clean the grouting between tiles, polish taps, and make sure the toilet is clean and the seat is down. Don't forget that the devil is in the detail. You're better off paying someone to come in and do a deep clean on your house than leaving it as it is and losing thousands when it comes to negotiating the sale.

Maintenance

The most common maintenance issue is interior wall cracks, especially in new-build properties as they take a few years to 'settle' after building. A little filler and some paint can solve the problem quickly and eliminate what may be an unstated concern from the buyer that your property is in poor condition or even suffering from subsidence.

They may not have said anything, in fact often the feeling may be subconscious, but it's important to ensure that the potential buyer feels an overall sense of emotional desire for your home and not worry too much about the price because they want it so much.

As in the example of the apartment on the previous page, sometimes this involves nothing more from the seller than a good tidy up and a lick of paint. Sometimes it means making sure unfinished DIY jobs are completed so the buyer doesn't end up with the wrong impression of the condition of the house and the amount of work involved in maintaining it.

In addition, you may want to think about repainting to neutralise garish colours or make the house feel fresher. Painting a ceiling white instantly makes a room feel lighter, brighter and bigger. When choosing paint, however, stick to pale colours, but don't use magnolia because it's such a cliché, and always remember to paint bathrooms and kitchens white – it makes them look clean and fresh.

Lighting

Make sure your interior looks welcoming. If it's a dark day, make sure all of your rooms are well lit and that you have a tidy entrance hall. Remember: first impressions really do count, and the hall is the first area viewers see.

Use ceiling spotlights to maximise the effect of the main selling points of the room. Daylight bulbs can brighten up dark and dingy places.

If you have a bathroom with no windows, always put the lights on before viewing and, just for the viewing, don't forget to turn off the fuse for the extractor fan. There's nothing worse than the drone of a noisy fan in a quiet house. Make sure you clean and polish mirrors carefully, too.

Never underestimate your viewers – they can be quite savvy. I know of one example of a north-facing flat on a ground floor. The sellers left doors open and daylight bulbs on, but the buyer knew to flick the lights off to see what the place really looked like. Unfortunately, the seller lost £5,000 off the asking price.

Dressing the house

You might want to rearrange your furniture to change the focus of a room (for example not have everything arranged around the TV) or create a space in the living room for a dining table if there is no separate dining room.

There are some very inexpensive things you can use to make your property look warmer, more inviting and home-like: try, for example, perfume bottles filled with water, pound shop jars filled with discount pasta, potpourri dishes, breadboxes, or cookie jars.

Keep rooms well ventilated, especially areas such as teenagers' bedrooms where bedding may not have been changed for ages, or rooms where pets spend a lot of time. This needs to be done regularly and well in advance; it's not enough to just open a window right before the viewing.

Curtains should always be clean and carefully arranged, and never fully drawn. Make sure venetian blinds are slatted in the right way. If you have a nice view, don't block it; if the view isn't particularly attractive, close your blinds or curtains (but not completely because then it's obvious you're trying to hide something).

The atmosphere in the house is also very important. For example, I had a hard-to-sell farmhouse – it was too quiet and depressing. Creating the right atmosphere can be achieved in the simplest of ways – we put the radio on in the background in the kitchen. During one viewing, I switched on The Archers. After all, it was a farmhouse!

Whatever you do, please don't smoke in the house. These days it is a definite no-no, even if your potential purchaser happens to smoke.

Even if your house is perfect, the buyer will always find something they don't like. In some cases, it might be worth having one thing that they can focus on and criticise so as not to attract their attention to other, potentially more serious, things that might detract more from the price of the house.

The garden

Neglected gardens can turn buyers off. I know of a cottage in Long Buckby that had an overgrown lawn but beautiful shrubs. We put decking outside the back door, stripped out the lawn and ordered a new one and the house sold within two weeks at near enough the asking price.

The client would not have been able to do this because they didn't know how to find a good, honest landscape gardener. Again, remember that your agent should be able to help you with contractors.

Viewings

A good estate agent will never conduct a viewing of a property they've never seen before; they should show up at least ten minutes early so that they can find their way around. Also, the agent should park their car out of the way, so as not to block access for the viewers.

Whoever is showing your house to viewers, they need to know how the central heating works, where all the keys are kept and so on. Therefore, they need to have a trusting relationship with the client so that the client feels comfortable giving out all this information.

You would feel uncomfortable having a neighbour showing buyers around your house, and you may not want to show people round yourself, either. A good estate agent or property coach is enough of a stranger so as not to embarrass you, but trustworthy enough to let into your house.

A seller can't really ask a buyer if they're in a position to buy, but an agent can; it's more impersonal. In addition, a good property coach or estate agent can spot potential problems before they happen whereas an independent seller doesn't have as much experience.

If you are showing viewers around your property, don't state the obvious (for example, "this is the master bedroom"). Also be aware of their body language for clues to help you figure out which rooms they like best. Then, when it's time for buyers to look at the house on their own, always go back to the room they liked best. It's not a good idea, either, for owners to follow the estate agent around during the viewing. In fact, it's best for you to go out and leave the expert to it.

Be careful what you say to buyers. Don't tell them you're moving because of negative equity or you need more space, or anything negative. And never discuss what you're going to leave behind in the house (such as cooker and carpets). Use the furnishings as a bargaining tool. The best answer is: "You'll need to speak to my agent/property coach about that."

Over the years, it's become clear that some clients need more guidance on presenting and selling a property than most estate agents are able to give. That's why I set up a completely separate service called mypropertycoach.

The theory behind property coaching is that you get unlimited guidance and help every step of the way. A coach will analyse your property and how it is presented compared to others in the area, and offer constructive advice and help on how to get it looking its best. They will talk you through lots of tips for getting your property to the top of the buyer's list and point out what isn't being done by your current estate agent that could be affecting your sale price and the time it takes to sell.

TOP TIPS ON PRESENTING YOUR HOUSE:

- Imagine who your buyer might be and present your house accordingly. For example, if they are a growing family, show spaces for children to play.

- Buyers make up their minds about a property within seconds of pulling up in front of it. Make sure the front of your house and its surroundings look so good that buyers can't wait to see inside.

- Once inside, don't disappoint them. Do everything you can to make your property light, spacious, clean and well presented.

- Whoever is showing buyers around your property needs to know about the central heating, where the keys are kept and so on. Buyers need to have their questions answered as quickly as possible.

SOLD!

subject to contract

CHAPTER 5
MARKETING YOUR PROPERTY

Marketing your property

Every property needs to have a tailored marketing strategy to stand the best chance of selling by attracting the right audience in the shortest time possible.

For example, a house valued at £150,000 is more likely to be marketed through the local press and online property search facilities (such as Rightmove.co.uk and other property websites) because the most likely buyers will be local people who like the area and want to upgrade their current house. On the other hand, a property valued above £400,000 – for example, in a canal-side location – requires a great deal more specialised marketing at local and national level.

Whatever the property, it needs to be marketed in a way that's guaranteed to get maximum exposure to the right audience. This includes newspaper and magazine advertising, high-street office window cards, the agency's own website and a strong presence on all of the main property portals (approximately 90% of all enquiries from buyers now originate through the internet).

These include:
www.primelocation.com
www.rightmove.co.uk
www.propertyfinder.com
www.propertylive.co.uk

In addition, agencies may make use of telemarketing, colour property details and, where necessary, colour brochures, location photographs, floor plans, video and virtual tours and aerial photos.

In my early days as an estate agent, I would take a photo of a house and then go to the local film processor down the road, and he would print me off a run of 7x5 inch prints. I'd then prepare the details for the house and stick the prints onto them. I'd be sitting there for hours sticking hundreds of photos onto sheets of A4 paper. It's not like that any more, thank goodness. Now it's all done by a digital printer. But I was the first estate agent to take my camera and start taking pictures of the inside of my clients' properties, however they looked. I used to tell a story by pictures – it is so much more effective.

I worked out that an estate agency's window should be like any other shop window. Pictures of just the front of houses are boring. I learned to dress the shopfront window with more interesting internal photographs and to change the properties on display more frequently. I learned very quickly that that was how to attract people to my window.

At the time, I was the only estate agent in Northamptonshire who even considered taking photos of the inside of somebody's house. I got business left, right and centre because of it. I used to deliberately put a cat or a dog in the picture, because the whole point was attracting people's attention. People would go: "Oh, look at that, there's a cat in the corner there!" That was my way of attracting them to that window and holding their attention.

And if you're ever outside an estate agency, remember they can hear everything you're saying on the other side of that glass. People say terrible things.

Don't prejudge them all – you have to give people a chance to prove themselves. The best one was a man talking to his wife. He had his nose pressed right up to the window looking at the pictures. As he walked away from the window, he said to his wife: "He's gonna take the shirt off my back." My instinctive reaction was to be angry, but then I thought no, now was my opportunity to shine. What a challenge. In he came – all aggressive – like a lot of people do. I was my usual jolly self and was determined that when this man left my office he held a different opinion of estate agents than the one he came in with.

He was in my office a good 30 minutes. I'd converted him. Not all estate agents are the same but most are very nice and pleasant, trustworthy and genuinely enjoy selling property.

I used to sit by the window listening to what people said. More often than not, there were some nice comments about the layout. So I learned very quickly how to dress a window by listening to customers' comments from the outside. I learned what works and what doesn't. Even now, my team still dress the window to impress.

What if you need to sell quickly?

If you need to sell your property really quickly, there are a number of ways your agent can help you. They can organise an open house where they invite as many people as possible on a particular day for a couple of hours to view your property (including the time-wasters). This creates a sense of excitement and urgency about your property and real buyers will be tempted to make an offer quickly.

There is also something called BMV – below market value, where your agent will find property investors who will buy your property and exchange contracts in a matter of days. As the name suggests, however, you will have to accept an offer well below the normal asking price.

Finally, there are property auctions where buyers will bid against each other for your property. Again, you may not achieve your asking price and, if you are in a hurry, this method of selling can take a bit longer than, say, a BMV.

Your agent should be highly flexible and be able to adopt different approaches depending upon circumstances. This is much more likely to generate opportunities that result in a sale than sticking rigidly to the 'traditional' methods of phoning potential buyers, advertising in the local press and putting the details up on Rightmove. These have their place in a marketing strategy, and we all use them, but they are by no means the only techniques available.

Particulars

Accurate, informative property details are fundamental to marketing your property efficiently.

What you don't want is a set of property details that skimps on information or has photos clearly taken with a stretch lens to make the rooms look larger. In addition, you don't want misdescriptions, such as calling an end terrace a semi-detached. And you most certainly don't want flowery language – a small and poky studio flat described as "compact, bijou and virtually maintenance free". "Needs some refreshing" really means "hasn't been touched since the 1970s – and that includes the inside of the toilet".

Giving misleading information directly contravenes the Property Misdescriptions Act. Furthermore, it is a fundamental problem that affects not only the sale price of a house but also the time it takes to achieve it. This is because the less a buyer knows and understands about your property before they visit, the more likely it is that your property won't match many of their criteria, leading to frustration for both them and you.

To ensure accuracy, these days estate agents use calibrated laser measures to give room dimensions in feet and metres. This data is entered into professional drawing software to produce plans from a simple floor plan to a 3D plan with a walk-through. You can also choose to have outline floor plans for illustrative purposes or more detailed floor plans with measurements of every aspect of the property, which is very useful if the property needs renovating.

At the same time as compiling these details, the agent should also visit and take photographs of your property. Your agent should be experienced at taking good photographs and understand the impact that light can have on the quality of the resulting images. They should therefore carefully evaluate the best aspects of your property, and the ones they know the buyers really want to see, and take the shots in the best possible light conditions.

Photography

Unfortunately, most estate agents are bad at taking photographs, which are often poorly composed and show unsightly items lying around that make the house look cluttered.

It's not uncommon to hear tales of trainee estate agents making some really basic mistakes when it comes to taking photos of a property. Wheelie bins in full view, cars on the driveway that obstruct part of the house (or worse the agent's liveried car strategically placed on the drive to get some free advertising), windows, front doors and garages left wide open and sometimes a kitchen with a sink full of dishes. It doesn't take much common sense to realise that these present the property in a bad light, not to mention embarrass the owner at the same time.

What you don't want are pictures taken with stretch lenses to make rooms and gardens look bigger (tip: look at how long the fences appear to be!) and the bare minimum of details designed to ensure the buyer has to book a viewing for a (usually unsuitable) property to find out more.

If the weather changes drastically, your agent should change the photos and take some new ones so they look as up to date as possible. If you live in an area of outstanding beauty or close to interesting landmarks or excellent local amenities, make sure there are photos of those as well. This could include railway stations, schools, parks, churches, bars and restaurants – whatever you think will attract your target market. I even take pictures of big supermarkets if I think it warrants it. Well, why not?

People want to see that they are buying much more than just your property; they are buying into a community and a lifestyle, so help them see what it would be like to live there by building a picture in their minds. With so many property details looking the same, having something different on yours will stop prospective buyers in their tracks and make them take a second look. Many agents focus almost exclusively on the property while forgetting that it's just one part of a much bigger picture.

In terms of content, your details should contain all the usual information, such as good clear room photos, descriptions and sizes, but there are also floor areas and floor plans, school catchment areas, council tax bands, energy efficiency and impact ratings, and occasionally aerial photos if the property comes with land or a number of outbuildings. Your details on the internet will need to include all of this, too, and there's the option to have virtual tours for those houses that need specialised marketing. The website can feature statistics about how many people have looked at your house, and include links to maps, Google Earth and street-view satellite photos.

Property descriptions also need to contain the right keywords and phrases, which a good agent or coach will know from experience are vital to increasing your visibility on the internet and being found quickly.

It is always important to focus on the benefits to the buyer in the property description. You might be proud of your expensive new kitchen, but the buyer may not care at all. One good exercise for the seller is to list the top ten benefits of living in the property from a buyer's perspective. For example, a family will want local schools, shopping (supermarkets), parks/playgrounds, plus spacious living accommodation, a large family kitchen and so on.

Ask your agent if you can put your own thoughts and feelings about your property in the details. If you are genuinely passionate about your property, why not tell your prospective buyers? Once your property details are complete, you should be sent a paper copy to check and give your seal of approval. If done properly, this could take several days because the agent should make absolutely sure that they have taken the best photos and compiled the details as accurately as possible. They shouldn't rush to get them to you in 24 hours and risk making silly mistakes or missing something vitally important.

Then the process of finding the right buyer begins!

Property websites or portals

One of the unfortunate characteristics of the internet is that the sheer amount of information uploaded every day means your property can quickly sink to the bottom of a pile. Many property portals have an option for buyers to only see properties that have been uploaded recently (usually within seven days), so after a cursory glance your property is then added to the 'seen' pile.

It is vital to extract it from this pile regularly and make sure it is continually under the eyes of the buyers. This could mean the agent or coach changing the description, the price, the photos, anything to keep your ad current. Just one simple change at the right time, such as a new photo of the house and garden from a different angle on a sunny day, could trigger interest in a buyer who may not have noticed it previously among all the other properties they've looked through. Ask your agent if they do this. If they don't, ask them to start doing it.

Finding the right buyers quickly

Your agent or coach will need to contact all the people they know who are looking for properties just like yours in the local area. Ideally, they will have all of their contact details, including mobile and home phone number and email address, so they can send the details in whatever format they prefer. It's important to have this because people's wants and needs change over time for various reasons and the agent will need to be able to update them quickly if property details change.

To find the right buyer in the shortest possible time, marketing needs to be undertaken in a methodical manner. The estate agent should have a database of thousands of potential buyers and should text, telephone, email or send a letter to everyone looking for a property like yours in your area. Potential buyers should be updated by email every week on new instructions and properties whose prices have altered.

An agent should start with buyers who have nothing to sell and can move quickly, such as first-time buyers living at home or in rented accommodation. They should then move on to the next group of buyers interested in your type of property who currently have their homes under offer or are awaiting offers, as they are the next group of people who could move quickly.

After that, they should contact those people with homes on the market with no offers. The final group are those buyers who have not yet started marketing their homes but who, for the right property, may be willing to do whatever is necessary to get their home on the market and sold quickly, such as drop their asking price or take out a bridging loan.

Qualifying a buyer

Once the agent has identified those people who may be interested, they assess them carefully to make sure they are serious about buying a property. Usually the agent makes sure they are serious before adding them to the database, but they should ask the relevant questions again in case their circumstances have changed. In addition, whoever calls as a result of having seen the property in the local papers or on the internet should also be checked out thoroughly.

For example, can they actually afford to buy a property and are they really interested in yours? Or are they merely 'rainbow chasers', or people who dream they can have a property as nice as yours and who spend weekends viewing properties but with no serious intention of buying anything?

My 20 years of experience have given me an instinctive feel for who is a serious buyer and who isn't. To start with, I ask a lot of questions. I don't exactly grill people, but I do make it clear that I want to know about them and their circumstances to make sure they're committed. If they want to buy a property, they will give me clear indications: they usually tell me why they are moving from their current place, what sort of finances they have in place and, most important of all, their full contact details. Rainbow chasers don't like giving out their contact details in case they get exposed for being time-wasters. Unfortunately, some agencies don't check as thoroughly.

And please don't be afraid if you are buying a property and a good agent does take an interest in you. That is an agent who knows what he or she is doing.

Once the buyers have proved themselves to be serious and your agent is confident they have the financial arrangements in place to buy your property, your agent should book them in for a viewing. It can take a little time to get all this organised. However, within a couple of weeks – if the agent has done their job properly – the viewings should start in earnest.

At the same time as contacting interested parties from their database, the agent should begin a tailored marketing campaign of your property to a wider audience in the local, regional or national press and media to gain the maximum possible exposure. This includes uploading your details onto online property websites, taking out newspaper and magazine advertising, and displaying your property details in their office window and on their website.

In some cases, there is a need for more bespoke, specialised marketing, such as full colour brochures, video and virtual tours, and aerial photos. Finally, to increase the chances of interest, a 'For Sale' board should be erected (unless you object) so anyone passing by can see that your property is on the market.

On the subject of 'For Sale' boards. I have heard every excuse possible for not having one. In my experience, the owner is really not serious about selling. In any market conditions, it's not about what you the seller thinks, it's about the buyer.

The buyer who is driving around your area will see that your house is for sale. The buyer who has your details in the car wants to find your property quickly. They haven't got time to run about trying to find you. Meanwhile, a property down the road has got a board outside and there's another opportunity lost.

By the way, if your reason for not having a board is that you don't want your neighbours to know, then it's probably too late. Good estate agencies are well known in any town so, if you have had three to five visits, it won't have gone unnoticed. Ask your agent for some cards and go and see your neighbours, whether you like them or not. Or, particularly if your property is empty, put a note through your neighbours' doors telling them this is the agency that will be dealing with your sale. When your prospective buyers pull up, at least you won't have the Neighbourhood Watch frightening them off. It does happen!

If you want to be taken seriously, make sure your agent places a nice clean 'For Sale' board outside your property.

Sending your details to the RIGHT prospective buyers

Many people complain about being sent property details that don't match their requirements or their price range. This is intensely irritating to sellers, not just buyers, as it demonstrates a lack of focused, targeted marketing of their property. However, there are some very good reasons why an agent may send a buyer details that don't always match all of their requirements. For example, the property may be:

- In a comparable area (in appearance, school catchment area or commuting distance) to the one you have requested, but have not yet considered;

- Of a higher specification than requested for the same money, that is, it may have an extra bedroom or study, or perhaps a bigger back garden;

- Missing one or more required features, but is in the right area and priced low enough for the buyer to add them later (for example, a property without a garage but with the room to build) and it's under the stipulated budget; or

- Exactly what the buyer is looking for space-wise, but for sale at a higher price. This happens when the buyer's budget doesn't match their requirements and the increased asking price works out at only a few pounds more a month when factored into a mortgage over a couple of decades.

However, if an agent sends you details for a new-build when you want a Victorian or Georgian character property, or you want a one-bed flat and the details sent are for a three-bed semi at twice the price, then they are flinging mud against a wall to see what sticks, usually because they can't be bothered to sift through their database to find the most interested buyers.

Accompanied viewings

Viewings are a prime opportunity for agents to make sure a buyer understands all the best features of your property, and to gauge their initial feelings towards what they are seeing. As most buyers hunt for properties after work, a good agent should be available seven days a week – including evenings – to ensure that potential buyers can quickly and easily request a viewing as soon as they see your property.

All viewings arranged through an estate agent should be accompanied. If your agent has a set of your keys, they should never simply hand them over and let a buyer into your property on their own. It's amazing that some agents still continue to do this knowing the security risks involved, apart from completely missing out on the most basic method of discovering the buyer's thoughts during a viewing and answering their immediate questions. I've even known buyers ready to make an offer right there and then. Wouldn't you want someone to be there if that happens?

The agent should also arrive at your home early to ensure everything is ready for the buyers. If you are at work at the time of the viewing, the agent should go around opening or closing curtains depending on the time of day, fluffing sofa cushions, turning on lights and generally familiarising themselves with your property's features once again. I've even been known to wash up if someone wasn't expecting a viewing and dashed off to work early that morning without doing it!

When the potential buyer arrives, the agent will take them on a tour of your house and garden, pointing out the features that match what they are looking for and why they think it would make a good home for them.

Experience of body language and psychology tells me whether a buyer is really interested and allows me there and then to draw out any questions or objections they may have, and overcome them. Once the viewing is complete, if you are not yet home, the agent should return your property to the way it was and then lock up securely.

Finally, every viewing should be followed up within 48 hours to find out what the buyer thought of your property. What were their expectations before they arrived and had those expectations been met? What other properties have they been to see that were comparable and how did yours stack up against them in terms of price and value for money? Whatever the feedback, positive or negative, the agent should share it with you and talk through any issues that may need addressing in light of the buyer's comments.

Your agent should do this with each and every buyer who views your home until they have secured you an offer.

Regular communication and feedback

Good communication is crucial from the beginning to the end of the sales process. It is frustrating not to be able to get an answer to a question quickly, so your agent should always be available; whether you phone or pop by the office, there should also be an experienced member of the team there to help you. An estate agent who leaves receptionists or new team members in the office alone is not doing their job properly. There should always be someone in the office who can deal with any of your queries or concerns.

Always do your research properly before choosing an agent. This will prevent problems, such as poor communication (for more information, see Chapter 3 on choosing the right estate agent or coach).

Your agent should provide you with regular feedback after viewings, pass on any offers – both verbally and in writing – keep you up to date throughout the negotiations and offer advice and guidance when you need it.

Once a price has been agreed, your agent should take charge of the sale through to completion, contacting you every week with a general update or immediately if it is urgent or requires your feedback. The sale should then move swiftly to a successful completion while you are fully informed every step of the way.

SOLD!

subject to contract

CHAPTER 6
WHAT HAPPENS WHEN YOU'VE ACTUALLY FOUND A BUYER?

What happens when you've actually found a buyer?

After a viewing, the prospective buyer will either give you an offer straight away or ask for more time to think about it. I have learned over the years to read a potential purchaser's body language and work out their intentions. I also ask them more questions to find out what I need to do to make them come back and offer the maximum price.

If the buyer puts in a low offer, I ask them to justify this by giving examples of comparable houses. If they can't give any real examples, then the price is unrealistic. I tell them that and say they need to be more reasonable.

After viewing, I go back to the seller and say: "I think we have a deal but we need to play it carefully." It is important for me to get the seller excited and talking about money so that they reveal their emotions. That way I can get a good idea of what the seller will take and the buyer will give and they will then try to reach a compromise.

Good negotiation techniques are vital in this process, so you can strike a good deal on price and timescales. At this point, it's the little things like fixtures and fittings that can make or break the deal. You need to be very clear about what you are leaving and what you are taking. For example, if a serious buyer is willing to offer you the asking price if you leave your beloved range cooker behind, it's well worth considering if it means you can obtain the maximum amount of money, move quicker and have less stress. Your agent should work with you to help you weigh up all the pros, cons and costs with each decision.

Millions of pounds every year are lost through poor property negotiations because people either cave in too quickly or feel insulted by a low offer and lose their cool with the buyer, who then goes elsewhere. It is possible to get more money from a buyer if you do your homework and ask the right questions during viewings. It's all about psychology and understanding people's limits.

You should receive any offers from buyers through your agent or coach immediately – both verbally and in writing – along with advice on the best course of action to take with each one. For example, can the buyer go ahead quickly? Do they have finance in place? How serious do they seem to be? Because all agents are required by law to pass on all offers, you shouldn't be alarmed if you receive low offers; they are a good starting point from which to negotiate upwards. But most importantly, you must feel that your agent is acting in your best interests.

Unless you're happy to just accept the first offer, or you love the bartering process, you need to have someone on your side to help with what can be a very difficult, even emotional, process. Once a price has been agreed, your agent should take charge of the sale and progress it through to completion, contacting you every seven to ten days with a general update or immediately if it is urgent or requires your feedback.

Finance

At this stage, it is important to check on the buyer's finances. Are they taking out a mortgage – and, if so, with whom? If they say they are a cash buyer, what exactly does that mean? Is the money available straight away or is it tied up in stocks and bonds? I've had a number of situations where, after further questioning, I've discovered that they aren't really cash buyers after all.

It is perfectly acceptable to ask for proof of finance, such as a copy of a bank statement. Every estate agent has the right to ask these questions as they are representing the seller in the negotiations.

Gazumping and gazundering

Gazumping is among one of the most difficult situations an agent will ever be caught up in. Estate agents are legally obliged to pass on every offer in writing under the Estate Agents Act 1979. Unfortunately, there is little an agent can do if a seller is determined to accept a higher offer after previously accepting a lower one and, once agents have passed offers on and offered advice and guidance, they cannot force sellers to ignore them, especially if they are being offered several thousand pounds more for their property.

While gazumping is a problem for a small percentage of sales, far more problematic, and on the increase, is gazundering. This is where a buyer will demand that a seller accepts a lower price at the time the contracts are about to be exchanged. In the current market, there may be a chance that the house value has dropped since the offer was accepted six to eight weeks previously, and the buyer wants to alter their offer as a result. Or perhaps a survey has revealed work that needs to be done on the house and the buyers are unhappy at having to spend that money after the sale. Alternatively, it could be because the buyers put in an offer above what they claimed they could afford in order to secure the property from other interested parties and are now worried by the financial commitment they have agreed to.

Unfortunately, whatever the reasons, there is no way to prevent gazumping or gazundering and each case will be different. In these situations, I would explain all the options available and help sellers decide the best course of action; your agent should be able to do the same. Fortunately, it doesn't happen that often, no matter what the media would have you believe, and I always try to dissuade buyers from doing it.

Surveys

Once you know your buyer has instructed their solicitor, it won't be long before a surveyor comes knocking at the door. You need to provide this surveyor with all the details they need to complete the survey and be available to offer them access to whatever parts of your property and garden they need to see. You may have to deal with the possibility of the selling price being renegotiated in light of new information that arises from the survey, and how you talk to your buyer at this point could hang the sale in the balance.

Surveys are designed to cover the surveyor so they cannot be held liable in the future. They are therefore usually positioned in a negative light, which can scare a buyer into thinking the worst. Your agent needs to be prepared to explain the implications of the survey, taking into account the concerns raised but keeping a sense of proportion.

For example, I had one sale where a structural survey said the 60-year-old roof may need replacing in the next few years. The word to note here is 'may'. In fact, it was obvious that the roof was in great condition for its age and would probably last another 20 years without problems if checked yearly for maintenance issues. The surveyor was covering himself for liability issues whether the roof needed replacing or not. The buyer's immediate reaction was that they'll have to spend £15,000 on a new roof and other highlighted issues in the next few years and was contemplating pulling out. With careful handling and further explanation, I was able to bring the buyer back on board.

All about HIPs

In 2007, the Government introduced Home Information Packs, or HIPs for short, in England and Wales in an attempt to reduce the time it takes for a property sale to be completed and reduce the incidence of sales falling through.

HIPs contain vital documents that a buyer needs to make a decision to buy your property and complete the sale, including evidence of title (that you own the property), standard searches (local authority enquiries, drainage and water, for example), an energy performance certificate (EPC) and commonhold and leasehold information (where appropriate).

An energy assessor will visit your property to collect the energy information required for the EPC part of the pack. This includes assessing the amount and quality of any double glazing, the thickness of the walls, how much cavity and loft insulation is present and what type of fuel and boiler you use to heat your home. Points are allocated to all these factors and the overall score will give you a very good indication of how cost-effective it is to heat, not to mention point out the quickest, most instantly effective ways to improve your rating.

HIPs may also contain a number of optional extras, such as a home condition report, and guarantees and warranties on any work undertaken or major appliances replaced, such as a central heating boiler.

Contacting all the relevant departments, booking energy assessments with inspectors, chasing suppliers to retrieve documentation and then putting everything together into a usable document can be a time-consuming and frustrating experience. I often help clients with this, and a good property coach will be able to do the same thing.

This is another area of selling your property where price is a direct indicator of quality. HIPs must achieve a certain standard to be considered legal and any company creating the HIP must be registered with the Property Codes Compliance Board (PCCB). This helps you differentiate between genuine firms offering a good standard of HIP and those that have sprung up to make a fast buck and aren't too concerned if their HIP doesn't make the grade. I always use Nigel Vokes from www.independentsolutionsuk.com.

Remember, you will always own your HIP and can take it with you if you decide to use another agent. Be careful that your agent doesn't tie you in with withdrawal fees or assume the copyright on the document. You have paid for it and it should be yours to keep.

Exchange of contracts and moving

When you reach exchange of contracts, you will need to book your removal team and arrange to have your utilities – such as gas, electricity and broadband – switched over to the new owners so that billing is their responsibility from the day they move in. You might also want to think about updating your will, to reflect your new circumstances, and ensuring you have enough insurance to cover your new home.

That's an awful lot to think about while you're packing up your own life. Do you have the time or even inclination to do all this and deal with the stress involved? Again, this is where a good agent or coach can help. They will be able to recommend or even arrange for someone to help you with all of this.

Other aspects of your move

In addition to selling your house, there are many other aspects to moving that will often fall outside of the remit of most estate agents. Nevertheless, people often need help with them given everything else that is going on. My philosophy is to help clients with all aspects of their move.

You will need to think about:

- Arranging a mortgage

- Legal services

- Conveyancing

- A HIP

- Property insurance

- Relocation services

- Removal companies

- Secure storage facilities

- Contractors, such as plumbers, plasterers, carpenters, tilers, electricians, a roofer and painters and decorators, as well as project management of these contractors if you are away or unable to do it yourself

- Property dressing

- Utility readings and connections – broadband, telephone, gas and electricity

- Key-holding – if you are away or on holiday

- Cleaning – general cleaning and specialised cleaning for carpets, curtains and upholstery

- Gardening and landscaping

- Property inspections

- Electrical and gas safety checks and servicing

- Pest control.

I have spent many years developing relationships with professionals and reputable local companies in these areas, making it much less stressful for clients than having to tackle some or all of these aspects themselves.

The most popular extra service I provide is making sure the utility meters are read, suppliers are changed and services, such as broadband and telephone, are connected ready for moving day. These are often the most irritating, time-consuming issues to sort out after you've moved.

SOLD!

subject to contract

CHAPTER 7
HOW TO BECOME A PROPERTY COACH

How to become a property coach

Property is at the forefront of everyone's mind these days – recent poor performances in pensions, stocks and shares and other types of investment vehicle have led many to the conclusion that bricks and mortar are the safest form of investment available today.

On numerous occasions throughout the book I have mentioned the concept of property coaching and I daresay that a number of readers will be thinking: "I fancy doing that." Being a property coach means being your own boss and being in charge of your own destiny. It also means you can work for yourself but not by yourself.

In addition, you can help prospective purchasers to realise a dream and to make a return on their investment and help sellers to find the right buyer for their property.

If you would like to find out more about my licensed associate programme, then take a look at my website – *www.campbell-online.co.uk* – and click on **Become an Associate**. No previous experience is required, just a keen interest in property and people. Full training will be given and support is continuously available.